D0844967

Spotlight on
ANCIENT CIVILIZATIONS
EGYPT

Ancient Egyptian
TECHNOLOGY

Leigh Rockwood

Published in 2014 by The Rosen Publishing Group, Inc.
29 East 21st Street, New York, NY 10010

First Edition

Editor: Jennifer Way
Book Design: Kate Vlachos
Layout Design: Colleen Bialecki

Photo Credits: Cover Pius Lee/Shutterstock.com; p. 4 Leoks/Shutterstock.com; p. 5 elena1110/Shutterstock.com; p. 6 Medioimages/Photodisc/Getty Images; p. 7 (top) Egyptian/The Bridgeman Art Library/Getty Images; pp. 7 (right), 13, 18, 20 DEA/G. Dagli Orti/Getty Images; p. 8 Bumihills/Shutterstock.com; p. 9 WitR/Shutterstock.com; p. 10 © 2001 Francis Dzikowski; p. 11 (top) Werner Forman/Universal Images Group/Getty Images; p. 11 (bottom) Danita Delimont/ Gallo Images/Getty Images; p. 14 bestimagesevercom/Shutterstock.com; p. 15 J.D. Dallet/age fotostock/Getty Images; p. 17 DEA Picture Library/De Agostini/ Getty Images; p. 19 Roberto Vannucci/E+/Getty Images; p. 21 Fedor Selivanov/ Shutterstock.com; p. 22 Nagib/Shutterstock.com.

Library of Congress Cataloging-in-Publication Data

Rockwood, Leigh.
 Ancient Egyptian technology / by Leigh Rockwood. – First edition.
   pages cm – (Spotlight on ancient civilizations: Egypt)
 Includes index.
 ISBN 978-1-4777-0768-5 (library binding) – ISBN 978-1-4777-0869-9 (paperback) – ISBN 978-1-4777-0870-5 (6-pack)
 1. Technology–Egypt–History–To 1500–Juvenile literature. 2. Egypt–Civilization–To 332 B.C.–Juvenile literature. I. Title.
 T27.3.E3R62 2013
 609.32–dc23
                                                     2013001128

Manufactured in the United States of America

CPSIA Compliance Information: Batch #S13PK2: For Further Information contact Rosen Publishing, New York, New York at 1-800-237-9932

CONTENTS

Ancient Egyptian Technology

Ancient Egypt is known for technology that was advanced for its time. Many of their inventions were things that helped them make the most of the Nile River's water. The Egyptian calendar was created to

Ancient Egyptians added sails to their boats around 2900 BC. This development in shipbuilding technology made it easier to transport heavy loads faster.

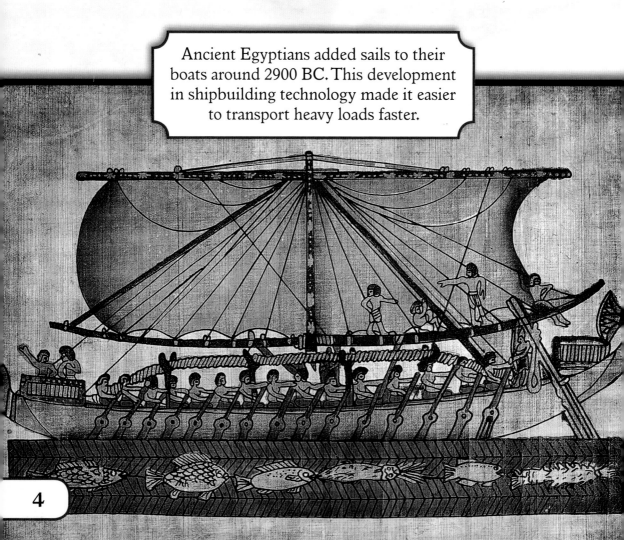

The Nile River, shown here, was important to ancient Egyptian civilization, including its technology.

keep track of the river's yearly flooding so that the Egyptians knew when to plant their crops. They also developed **irrigation** systems to move water from the river to the fields.

Ancient Egyptians used shipbuilding technology to build boats to transport goods along the Nile. These boats carried the heavy building materials used to build Egypt's **tombs**, temples, and pyramids. Many of these structures are still standing today!

Building Tools

Ancient Egyptian building tools were made of copper, **bronze**, and basalt. They were simple chisels, drills, and picks, but they were strong enough to cut blocks of stone to build pyramids, tombs, and temples.

The Temple of Luxor, shown here, was built thousands of years ago and still stands today.

Above: This wall carving shows two sculptors using their tools to carve a statue.
Right: This is a selection of ancient Egyptian carpentry tools.

Stonecutting and carving tools were used to break off blocks of stone in rock **quarries** in the desert and to shape them into smaller pieces. Then the rocks were put on a large sled that could carry loads of up to 2.5 tons (2.3 t). It took as many as 100 men to pull the sled to the river. From there, a boat carried the rocks to wherever they needed to go.

The Pyramids

The ancient Egyptian religion placed a great deal of importance on the afterlife. The Egyptians built huge stone tombs called pyramids to house and protect the bodies and belongings of their **pharaohs** and other important people.

The Pyramid of Djoser is also called the Step Pyramid. It is the most famous example of an early ancient Egyptian pyramid.

The pyramids of Giza, shown here, are examples of later, smooth-sided pyramids.

The Pyramid of Djoser is the oldest pyramid in ancient Egypt. It was built around 2600 BC for the pharaoh Djoser. This pyramid looks like a set of giant steps made of pieces of rock. As their building technology improved, ancient Egyptians developed a method of building pyramids using larger blocks. These pyramids had smooth, flat sides that met at a point at the top.

Technology and the Nile

The Nile's yearly flooding provided water for ancient Egyptian farms. As the number of farms grew, they needed to move this water over a larger area. They developed irrigation systems to control where the water went.

These workers are preparing the soil and planting seeds. Irrigation technology allowed ancient Egyptians to move water from the Nile to their farms. Irrigation also allowed them to increase the number of farms they could water.

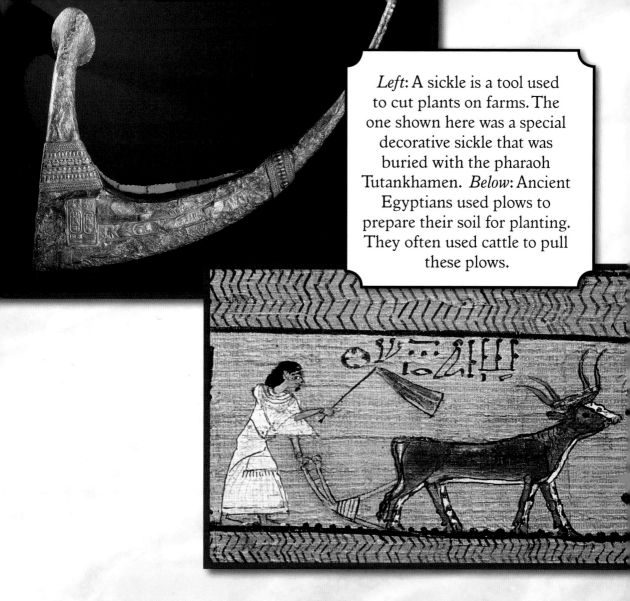

Left: A sickle is a tool used to cut plants on farms. The one shown here was a special decorative sickle that was buried with the pharaoh Tutankhamen. *Below*: Ancient Egyptians used plows to prepare their soil for planting. They often used cattle to pull these plows.

First, they used hoes to dig holes to trap water. Then they dug **canals** to lead the water to dry land. They also built walls out of mud to keep water from flowing to places where they did not want it to go. By using this irrigation technology, ancient Egyptians were able to grow more crops to feed their growing population.

Transportation in Ancient Egypt

Shipbuilding was an important development in transportation technology in ancient Egypt. The civilization's first boats were rafts made from stalks of the papyrus plant that had been tied together. These light boats were used to move food and goods along the Nile. Rafts did not have sails. Instead, they moved using the river's **current**.

By 2900 BC, ancient Egyptians had improved their shipbuilding technology by developing sails, which used the wind to carry boats quickly through the water. They also began building wooden boats. These newer boats were strong enough to carry heavy stone blocks, as well as to travel at sea.

The Khufu ship is one of the world's oldest, biggest, and most-intact ships. This ship may have carried the pharaoh Khufu's body to his burial site. The boat was then buried there so the pharaoh could use it to visit the Sun god Ra in the afterlife.

The Egyptian Calendar

The ancient Egyptians used the Nile's regular flooding to develop their calendar. Around 2800 BC, they calculated that the river flooded about every 365 days. They then based their calendar on this cycle. They further divided their calendar into 12 months. This was based on the changes in the Moon's appearance, which went through 12 cycles per year.

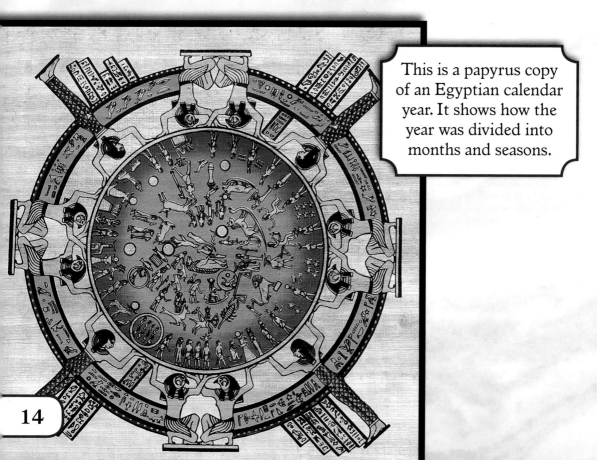

This is a papyrus copy of an Egyptian calendar year. It shows how the year was divided into months and seasons.

The ancient Egyptian calendar was tied to the regular cycle of flooding of the Nile River. Here, the Nile has flooded near the city of Luxor, Egypt.

Farmers used the calendar to know when they should irrigate their land and when they should plant their crops. Ancient Egyptians grouped their year into three seasons, based on their farming cycle. The Nile flooded in the spring. In winter, the floodwater began to dry up. Summer was the driest season.

Telling Time

Ancient Egyptians came up with different technologies to tell time. One was the sundial. A stick was placed in the ground at the center of a circle. As the Sun moved, the shadow created by the stick moved, showing the time of day.

The water clock was invented so that people could measure time. Two pots were placed on top of one another. The top pot had a hole in the bottom. It was filled with water. As water dripped into the lower pot, a person measured how much time had passed by reading the markings on the inside of the top pot.

Here is a copy of an ancient Egyptian water clock. The water clock was marked so that the Egyptians could tell how much time had passed. The water dripped into a pot below through a small hole in the bottom of the pot.

Medicine in Ancient Egypt

Ancient Egyptians used technology to make important medical discoveries. They made medicines from plants. They also developed methods to treat injuries, such as using splints to set broken bones. They developed tools for surgery, such as knives, scissors, and **scalpels**.

This wall carving shows a doctor treating a man who is using a crutch. Ancient Egyptian doctors could treat injuries like broken bones using splints made of wood padded with cloth.

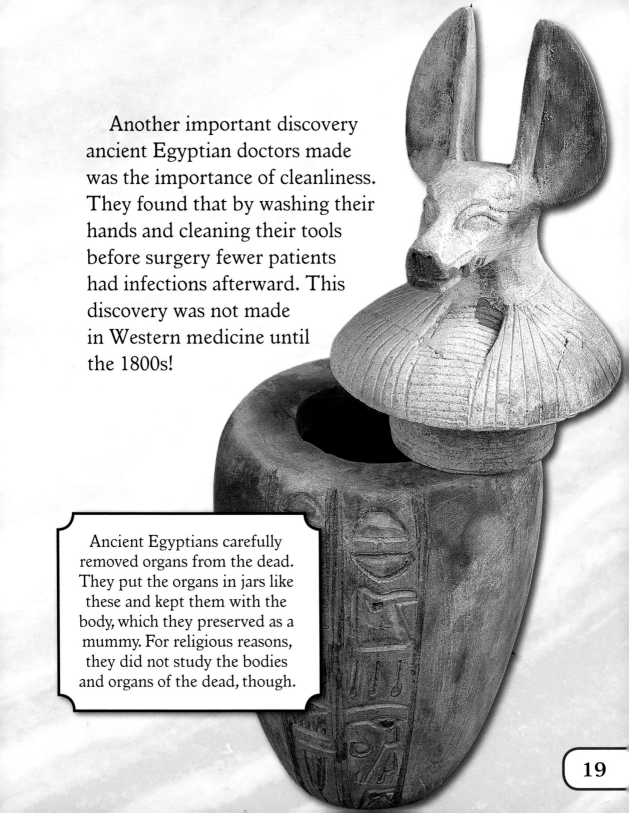

Another important discovery ancient Egyptian doctors made was the importance of cleanliness. They found that by washing their hands and cleaning their tools before surgery fewer patients had infections afterward. This discovery was not made in Western medicine until the 1800s!

Ancient Egyptians carefully removed organs from the dead. They put the organs in jars like these and kept them with the body, which they preserved as a mummy. For religious reasons, they did not study the bodies and organs of the dead, though.

Hieroglyphics and Paper

Ancient Egyptians invented **hieroglyphics,**
which was one of the world's first writing
systems. Hieroglyphics are picture symbols.
They were first developed so that pharaohs
could keep track of their land and keep records.

This wall carving shows scribes at work
writing hieroglyphics on papyrus. Scribes
were the people who were taught to write as
their trade in ancient Egypt.

Here is an example of Egyptian hieroglyphics carved into stone.

Hieroglyphics were also carved onto the walls of tombs and temples to tell stories about the gods and the lives of pharaohs and other important people.

Hieroglyphics were also written on papyrus paper. Ancient Egyptians made this paper with the stalks of the papyrus plant. The invention of papyrus paper gave ancient Egyptians a way to keep records and record their history and their discoveries.

Learning from Others

Ancient Egyptians also **adapted** technology from other cultures. There were few wars in the early centuries of Egyptian civilization, and their weapons were simple and made of wood. When the Hyksos began **invading** Egypt around 1650 BC, the Egyptians adapted the Hyksos' weapons technology. The Egyptians began to make weapons from bronze rather than wood. They developed **chariots** that improved on the Hyksos design. Although it was a difficult period, Egypt emerged from it as a stronger, more technologically advanced civilization that lasted another 1,300 years.

Here, the pharaoh Ramses II rides a chariot. Ancient Egyptians built chariots that improved on the Hyksos' design.

GLOSSARY

adapted (uh-DAPT-ed) To have changed to fit new conditions.

bronze (BRONZ) A golden brown blend of copper and tin metals.

canals (ka-NALZ) Man-made waterways.

chariots (CHAR-ee-uzts) Two-wheeled battle cars pulled by horses.

current (KUR-ent) The flow of water in one direction.

hieroglyphics (hy-ruh-GLIF-iks) A form of writing that uses more than 700 pictures for different words and sounds.

invading (in-VAYD-ing) Entering a place to attack and take over.

irrigation (ih-rih-GAY-shun) The carrying of water to land through ditches or pipes.

pharaohs (FER-ohs) Ancient Egyptian rulers.

quarries (KWOR-eez) Areas of land where stones for building can be found.

scalpels (SKAL-pools) Small, light, usually straight knives used in surgical and anatomical operations and dissections.

tombs (TOOMZ) Graves.

INDEX

WEBSITES

Due to the changing nature of Internet links, PowerKids Press has developed an online list of websites related to the subject of this book. This site is updated regularly. Please use this link to access the list:
www.powerkidslinks.com/sace/tech/